How Do Monster Trucks Work?

Buffy Silverman

Lerner Publications • Minneapolis

Lerner Publications Company
A division of Lerner Publishing Group, Inc.
241 First Avenue North
Minneapolis, MN 55401 USA

For reading levels and more information, look up this title at www.lernerbooks.com.

Library of Congress Cataloging-in-Publication Data

Silverman, Buffy, author.
    How do monster trucks work? / Buffy Silverman.
       pages cm — (Lightning bolt books. How vehicles work)
    Summary: "Young readers will love this exciting, in-depth yet accessible look at monster trucks, including how they work, the special equipment they need, and how they crush puny cars under their enormous tires"—Provided by publisher.
    Includes bibliographical references and index.
    Audience: 5–8.
    Audience: K–3.
    ISBN 978-1-4677-9499-2 (lb : alk. paper) — ISBN 978-1-4677-9683-5 (pb : alk. paper) — ISBN 978-1-4677-9684-2 (eb pdf)
    1. Monster trucks—Juvenile literature. I. Title.
TL230.15.S555 2015
629.223'2—dc23
                                          2015017448

Manufactured in the United States of America
4-49848-20612-11/18/2020

Table of Contents

What Is a Monster Truck?

A monster truck speeds up a ramp. It launches into the air. It soars over three cars!

Most trucks are made to stay on the ground. But monster trucks are built to leap and bounce. They race around tracks against other monster trucks.

These monster trucks are racing against each other.

A worker puts a tire on a monster truck.

The first monster trucks were made from pickup trucks. People added huge tires and more powerful engines. They put bigger springs on the wheels to help the trucks bounce.

Monster trucks used to weigh more. The parts that made up the trucks were heavier. Modern monster trucks are made of parts that are strong and light. Being light helps them go fast and soar!

Even with lighter parts, modern monster trucks can still crush cars!

A monster truck must be able to make bumpy landings. It needs a strong frame. The frame supports the body and the engine. The frame is made of light steel tubes.

This truck's frame is red.

Monster Power

It takes a lot of power to make a giant monster truck zoom. The truck's engine turns fuel into power that makes it go.

This is a monster truck engine. Monster trucks are lighter than they once were, but they still need lots of power!

Monster truck engines make smoke when they burn fuel.

A monster truck's engine is huge. It uses more fuel than most truck engines.

Fuel needs oxygen from air to burn. A fan brings air into the engine. A monster truck engine needs lots of air so it can burn more fuel.

Workers repair monster truck engines and keep them running.

Inside the engine are pistons.
There are usually eight pistons.

These are pistons.

A piston sucks in air as it goes down. Fuel is sprayed inside the tube. The piston goes up and squeezes the air and fuel. A spark lights the fuel. It explodes and pushes the piston down. Then the piston goes back up.

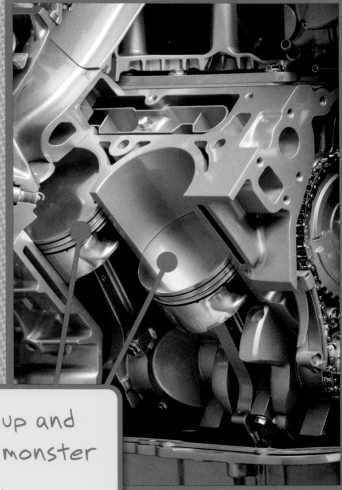

Pistons move up and down inside a monster truck engine.

Pistons turn the crankshaft.

The pistons are connected to a crankshaft. The crankshaft turns when the pistons go up and down. The crankshaft makes the monster truck's wheels turn.

Giant Tires

Monster trucks can plow through deep mud with their big tires. Most monster truck tires are 66 inches (168 centimeters) tall. That's taller than some adults.

A monster truck's tires spread the truck's weight over a big area. The tires do not sink. The truck speeds across muddy ground.

A monster truck's tires are not fully pumped with air. Soft tires are less likely to burst on a big landing.

This monster truck bounces on its big tires.

Moving tires rub against the ground. Rubbing is called friction. Friction lets tires grip the ground. Friction also slows a monster truck.

This monster truck sends dirt and rocks flying.

Monster truck tires are heavy. A bit of each tire is shaved off before a race. This helps the monster truck weigh less.

These monster truck tires are ready to race!

Built to Bounce

When a monster truck hits a big bump, the ground pushes the wheels up. Then gravity pulls the wheels down. This can make for a rough ride.

Springs and shock absorbers keep the body and frame of monster trucks from bouncing too much. The springs attached to the wheels move up and down as the wheels bounce. The springs move instead of the rest of the truck.

Do you see the springs on this monster truck?

Shock absorbers slow the bouncing springs. A shock absorber looks like a bike tire pump. It is filled with gas. One end is attached to the truck's frame and the other to a wheel.

These are shock absorbers.

A rod moves inside the shock absorber when the truck bounces. The rod pushes against the gas. The rod and gas slow the bouncing springs.

Driving the Monster

A driver climbs into a monster truck cockpit. She puts on her helmet. She straps on seat belts. She pulls the starter switch. The engine roars.

This monster truck driver is ready to roll!

The driver turns the steering wheel, and the front wheels move. She flicks a switch, and the back wheels turn. The driver can make a tight turn by turning all four wheels.

The driver steps on the gas.
The truck zooms onto a ramp.
The front of the truck points up.

Grave Digger
is taking off!

Grave Digger flies through the air. Monster trucks soar higher than any trucks in the world!

Diagram

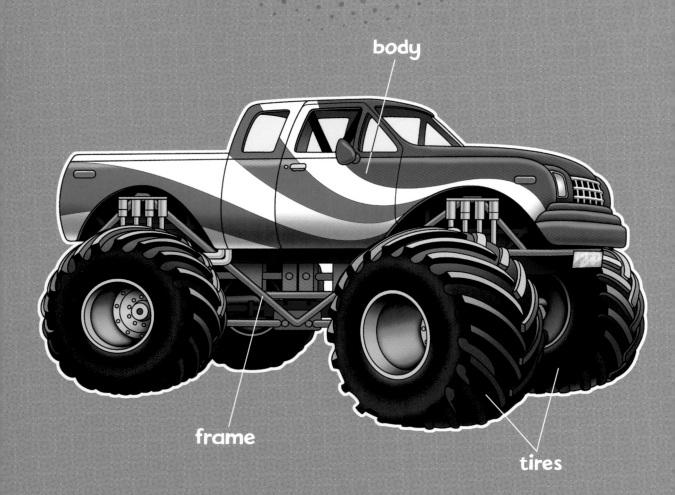

body

frame

tires

Monster Truck

Fun Facts

- The world's fastest monster truck drove more than 99 miles (159 kilometers) per hour. It needed a lot of fuel to go that fast. It used about 1 gallon (3.8 liters) of fuel to drive 264 feet (80 meters)!

- Monster trucks may flip and crash during a show. Their frames break. Tires pop. The trucks' bodies are dented. Workers fix the trucks before the next show.

- Many monster truck drivers build their own trucks. They start with the body of a normal truck. Then they add new parts to turn it into a monster!

Glossary

body: the main outside part of a monster truck

engine: a machine that gives monster trucks power to move

frame: the metal parts that hold a monster truck's body and engine

friction: the rubbing of one object against another

gravity: a force that pulls objects down

piston: a part of an engine that moves up and down and makes other parts move

shock absorber: a tool connected to the wheel of a vehicle that slows bouncing springs

spring: a metal piece that can return to its shape when it is pressed or pulled

Further Reading

Bigfoot—Monster Trucks
http://bigfoot4x4.com/blog/?page
/id=295

Brecke, Nicole, and Patricia M. Stockland.
Cars, Trucks, and Motorcycles You Can Draw.
Minneapolis: Millbrook Press, 2010.

Goodman, Susan E. *Monster Trucks!* New York:
Random House, 2010.

How to Draw a Monster Truck
https://www.youtube.com/watch?v=UIyEuyomEzE
#t=79

Kids Truck Video—Monster Truck
https://www.youtube.com/watch?v=uLbBx_25y3U

Index

Photo Acknowledgments

The images in this book are used with the permission of: © Natursports/Shutterstock.com, p. 2; U.S. Air Force/Lance Cheung, p. 4; © Michael Doolittle/Alamy, pp. 5, 16, 24; © PCN Photography/Alamy, pp. 6, 9, 20, 22; © Margaret Norton/NBC/NBCU Photo Bank via Getty Images, p. 7; © iStockphoto.com/caelmi, p. 8; Anton Novoderezhkin/ZUMA Press/Newscom, p. 10; © Jim Damaske/Tampa Bay Times/ZUMA Wire/Alamy, p. 11; © iStockphoto.com/rasslava, p. 12; © iStockphoto.com/MPKphoto, p. 13; © iStockphoto.com/alex-mit, p. 14; © Peter Albrektsen/Shutterstock.com, p. 15; Juan DeLeon/Icon SMI/Newscom, pp. 17, 18, 23, 25; © Silvia Blaszczyszyn Jakiello/Dreamstime.com, p. 19; © Transtock/SuperStock, p. 21; © Alan Ashley/Southcreek/ZUMAPRESS.com/Alamy, p. 26; AP Photo/Bizuayehu Tesfaye, p. 27; © Laura Westlund/Independent Picture Service, p. 28; Terry Harris/REX Shutterstock/Newscom, p. 30.

Front cover: © Photo courtesy of Dan Patrick Enterprises, Inc.

Main body text set in Johann Light 30/36.